Acknowledgements

Grateful acknowledgement is made to the Ontario Arts Council for its financial support for this project. The encouragement and support of Marty Gervais and his publishing company, Black Moss Press, are also acknowledged with thanks.

Poems in this collection have appeared in **Canadian Author, Envoi** (Wales), **iota** (England), **Orisha** (Canada), **Poemata** (Canada), **The Tanglewood Trib** (Canada) and **The Windhorse Review** (Canada).

Quarry, Husk, Winter Dawn, and *The Endless Blue* were published in both German and English versions in **Geschriebene Bilder** (M & N Boesche Verlag, Berlin & Haifa, 1990).

Special thanks are extended to Maria Jacobs, Carol Malyon, Michael Wurster, Gilda Mekler, and Leslie Nutting. Without their critical advice on the manuscript, these poems might never have attained book publication.

Cover art by Gilda Mekler.

NOTES

The quotation in *Into Light* is from **Gates of the House, The New Union Home Prayerbook** (Central Conference of American Rabbis, New York, 1977).

The Marcus Aurelius quotation in *A Winter Birth* is from **Thoughts,** translated by John Jackson (Oxford University Press, 1906).

The Loyalists mentioned in *Hawk, Witness,* and *Triptych* are the United Empire Loyalists. The Loyalists and their children, including one Simon Deahl, moved to Canada following the American Revolution. They were the first English-speaking settlers in the valley of the Thames.

ISBN 1 874161 13 5

13/4/94

ENVOI POETS PUBLICATIONS

CONTENTS

THE BALANCE

Like a twig caught
    by an eddy
the Great Bear
    circles Polaris.

Seeing such
    constancy
it's possible to
    imagine paradise —

to imagine stars
    in near vacuum
speaking a tongue
    without sin.

Omnivorous,
    living in blackness,
tiny bonfires
    to steer by,

a path set out
    through dark waters
for sailors to dream
    and follow.

NOVEMBER

Cast-down maple leaves
lie in a yellow pool
spread on thin grass;

the flare of sumac
cresting its hill
is a signal
warning of winter gales.

Already cold winds rise;
leaves dot the river
like distant suns.

ON THE PRAIRIES

On the Prairies
cold November rains
fall into the open ground.
They shift across fields
where grain once rose
proud in its harvest coat.

From deep porches
farmers scan bleak skies
for signs of the first snow;
and winter comes
redemptive in its purity,
in its sharp steel.

HUSK

After the first hard frost
farmers enter upon their frozen land
to bring in the year's feed corn.
Along rough county roads

draught horses plunge in heavy air,
forged shoes striking congealed ruts.
Stalks rustle in the wind's teeth
brittle with the scent of snow.

Through the long dusk the grain
is dragged by solitary workmen
to barns that lean red
into the blood of a harvest sky.

All autumn the men go
silent among the ragged trees that
mark off field from hand-worked field.
Stiff with sleep they dream of corn,

dream of that bullet of frost
lodged in the heart of every kernel,
of the dead weight of each iron
ear in the shucking hands.

TANGLEWOOD ORCHARD

I

After weeks of dry weather
snow builds its white house
in the summer bower.

II

Far to the west, quicksilver clouds
blot out our distant sun;
the last leaves rattle their bare trees.

III

Cardinal and blue jay
decorate scrub and hedgerow —
the only colour to touch the woods this season.

IV

I cast out crusts for birds and rodents.
Dark smoke rises into the sunset;
I open the door to the winter.

V

All night going home
the wind carries bits of light
into morning's bright hive.

HAWK

Late November.
A white stillness
spreads
field to field

cows wander
with heavy breath
searching through
frozen stubble
for overlooked corn.

In the cemetery
Loyalist graves
two centuries old

the struggle
for harvests,
for children,
for their hard
cold land.

The winter hawk
glides
looking for mice

its rich brown
is set against
the grey
of banked storm clouds
stretching
to Lake Huron
and beyond.

INTO LIGHT

for Shona Deahl

You are pushed into light by the dark body
as it convulses in its cave of pain.
I hear your thin wail and grunt
as streamers of blood are wiped away and
you are carried off by the midwife
to be weighed and wrapped.

Outside lies the stilled night.
Venus crosses the border into Virgo;
soon snow will streak our sky.
I lift the book and read: "Bestow
Your blessing on our child, that she may grow
in strength of body, mind, and spirit.
May she learn to love all that is good
and beautiful and true."

Goddess of Spring, Goddess of Justice,
seeker of life and truth, whose darkness
will your love-light soften? Whose word
will quicken your heart to compassion
before our nights grow long?

For only death is certain
and we are like mad explorers
trudging further north under winter's triangle.
Yet tears of joy grace every cheek.
In the bright room we form a ring of life,
lurch drunk on sleeplessness
into the luminous folds of a fresh dawn.

A WINTER BIRTH

for Simone Deahl

The works of God
   are full of providence;
The works of Fortune
   are not independent of Nature ...
Thence flow all things.
Marcus Aurelius

With a twist of forceps
you are delivered into a life
where deliverance, if it comes,
comes with that final dark
far from the bright lights
of this incandescent room.

Though darkness fills
the cracks that edge our days,
we celebrate your first week
by lighting candles,
let the Menorah
illuminate our lives,
a festival of joy in yours.

Home early from work,
I hold you to a window
to catch the last December light,
watch while our sun sets
in its prison of ice.
I know I cannot save you
from life's pain.

All things flow
and you grow into spring.
In green shade I walk
through the fortunate dark
of new buds. I'm shaped
to your stillpoint,
the immense world moving
ponderous around us.

QUITE EARLY CHRISTMAS MORNING

Quite early Christmas morning
the Herdsman rises in the east
to stand over the stripped branches
of poplar and oak. Below his waist
swings an orange lantern
to light the way for the coming dawn.

The town's shut tight;
the sky between Arcturus and
Spica wears its black mask.
Snow hides in the roots of dark trees
while above the river, mist ghosts
cast halos about the streetlamps.

Wise men have long understood
light consumes the terrors of our night,
and so these constellations
swing above our heads —
each a bright song sung
in darkness waiting.

WITNESS

Snow swept in today
to bury the browns
of a winter's afternoon.

These are the vast storms
born far in the wheat-lands.
They cross a thousand barren miles
to reach these lowland fields.

A century and a half past
the first Loyalists
entered this valley.

Here they founded an Anglican church,
raised a building
to house an Orange Lodge,
set out their cemetery.

I have seen their stones
leaning white into
the whiteness of Prairie storms.

POEMS FOR A WINTER RIVER

I

All day your grey waters carry rafts of ice
to Lake St. Clair and Detroit
as the year closes.

II

In the heart of the marshland
dry reeds whisper their grief
to the winter wind.

III

I wander the river bank
lost in a hundred shades of brown
as bells summon the faithful to mass.

IV

The evening lights
its dark lamp
in an empty heron's nest.

V

I follow the south fork home;
the radiant Twins overhead are unmoved
by the *canto negro* of the river at night.

WINTER DAWN

Out of the east
    a cold snow;
in country fields
    lying beneath grey mist
ice flowers bloom
    among dry corn stubble.

The land is open
    and white
pierced only
    by black trees
stripped bare by weeks
    of heavy frost.

The great silence
    of early dawn
covers farm and woodlot
    — even the old rooster
dares not speak
    to the apple tree today.

TABLEAU

Not a leaf is left
on the poplars
where they stand locked
in their frozen pools.

Behind their boughs
winter turns the sky to silver
as daylight darkens
over an icy river.

Deep in the floodplain
nothing moves
save a man and his dog
silently walking the iron ground.

JANUARY THAW

After a month of snow
an unexpected thaw —
the river rose,
                    spilled over
its banks
    all the way to clay bluffs.

The path to town washed out
I stay home,
                watch cold water
swirl through branches
where last week
    black squirrels raced.

THE ENDLESS BLUE

Among leafless trees
    scattered jack pines
go scraggly in wind.
    The brook lies quiet
under its skin
    of ice.

A deepening red
    creeps along the canes
of the raspberries.
    At the edge
of the escarpment
    snow clings to blank rock.

All around me
    a hard clarity.
And I am happy
    for the sharp skies,
for the endless blue
    of heaven.

LIGHTING THE DARK INTO SPRING

Through April's icy days
farmers burn dead branches
cut from orchards or scarred windbreaks.

The smoke of many fires
fills dark afternoons, drifts
over fields of frozen stubble.

Suddenly the deep frost leaves
and boys on bicycles race
along the rutted roads —

their shouts ignite the bonfire dusk.

THREE TINY SPRING POEMS

Near the creek
bur oak stand knee-deep
in their reflections.

At the millrace
shadows of dove and killdeer
touch cold water.

Fieldstone house —
martins nest
under dark eaves.

SPRING RAIN

Morning brings a dampness into the orchard. Throughout the woodlot, branches of northern hardwoods shine in their black skins. Early spring — faint green begins to outline the crowns of wild cherry and aspen. Maple blossoms, brought down last night, speckle the path.

The rain starts again, drifting in sheets across yard and pasture. I go down by the lake where silence has soaked into the beds where reeds sleep. In the lake's black corridors solitary fish seek the deepest spots. All day water falls into water.

Land fresh from the turning ploughs thickens with mud. Soon I can no longer be sure if this voice I hear belongs to the rain or the opened fields. When night advances from its house in the east, our sky becomes luminous like still waters deep in hidden wells or the first blood of a waking heart.

TWO PIECES FOR SPRING

By late April the rains cease;
rivers return to old channels
leaving pools that reflect
fresh green buds.

. .
. .

Under spring constellations
winds sweep the great oaks;
we walk near dark waters
with no need to speak.

RETURN

Early in May a soft wind
slips unnoticed from the south
to set our forsythia free,
unlock the lavish magnolias
brimming pink and silver.

All over town
trees open their green day,
a flush creeps branch to branch
where warm sun breathes.

Wild grasses return from their knitted roots
as moisture rises
to find that level where
life begins.
                    And suddenly I stand
gazing into the white
heart of spring.

APPLE TREE IN SPRING

Completion comes
to the apple tree in spring.

The sun, closer now,
joins its shining hoop;

even my old glove,
lost so long ago,
returns.

The mountain of light
opens
                and every particle
flows out —
a river of silver
washing the blossoms

white to white
to rose.

THE GARDEN

The wind in the garden
wanders among fallen lilacs.

It comes like a dark whistle from night's hollow bone,
across plains where hands of wood
bury seeds while our moon hangs swollen.

Years pass
and I'm reminded of Nebraska —
how winter snows drift
thoughtlessly into the east.

Little by little my grief
is carried off,
is freed from its weight of stone flowers;

and I too wander
joyous at last
into the cold light
of stars.

NORTHERN TRAINS

Deep in the quiet hours
unseen locomotives call.

I hear them lonely
beyond my garden's black cloak,

lonely throughout the nights
of small dark towns.

They whistle along an Ontario Northland spur
where summer opens

like the mouth of a child
already learning to say goodbye.

INDIGO BUNTING

The indigo bunting
      is a flash of blue
iridescent among new leaves
    where the path verges
      on cool water.

His flight moves like blue flame
      through shadows so dense
the river's voice
    barely pierces
      their green silence.

THE TASTE

A morning so fresh the sun shines like
a school of minnows flashing through pure water.
My daughter climbs a willow; small bare toes
grip bark ridged and furrowed with age.

Later, Simone wades that moist edge
where land becomes lake. She chases baby catfish
through cool shallows, her world instant and direct,
each moment luminous with her joy or anger.

Lunch time comes. Across a wooden bench we spread
cheese, oranges, bread, and wine.
On the back of my tongue a single crimson drop
recalls the hand-worked cask.

I taste oak staves, hours of sunlight,
the dusky shadows of vines where vineyards run down
to the sea. The wine holds a sharp fruitiness
tossed, like a child's laughter, fresh in the mouth.

BRIM

I

Kingfishers flash away and back
a wing-beat above this pond
swollen with last night's downpour.

II

Year of freakish summer rains;
creeks overflow into fields
their rich mud swamping the young corn.

III

My daughter naps on a blanket that once was mine.
Not far away, a muskrat patrols
the brim of her watery world.

IV

Baby, man, muskrat —
our very world passes away
in a blink, in an instant.

V

Willows weep into the pond,
their branches deep in the risen waters
where green and its green echo are one.

SIMONE AT THE RIVER

All season the sun pours
its light into the Thames.
Carp feed and grow
to crest in a world of reeds and silt.

And crested they surge from cool mud
to flicker golden on the surface.
They pass like silent flames
through blue shadows
and are gone.

Your face as you look
into the river's wet dark
is also golden.
It's a child face,
precious beyond measure.

Out of your mouth
come shining words —

"Fish"
"Water"
"Swim"

— fleeting as flecks
of sunlight
where the waters lie wrapped
in their blue layers.

QUARRY

At the centre
of a cornfield
lies a gravel deposit;

smoothed rocks
hidden by a glacier
twenty thousand years ago.
Place where

our land's stone heart
is laid bare to the
empty sky;

where at dusk
clouds and mist return
to their haven
under the earth.

MIDSUMMER EVE

After lovemaking
        the wind enters
the dark heart
            of the aspens,
Heaven's River
        summons a new season.

A DOOR IN THE WATER

Across miles of cornfields
we come at last to a lake where
the blue of a Midwest sky
enters the darker blue
of deep waters.

Everywhere lies the still hand
of summer, the sweep
of space without measure.
Footstep by footstep
we leave the details of our world.

In the yellowing tassels
a time of mourning. In the
breeze through the arched leaves
the sound of mystery.
Far to the west, beyond the

mountains we cannot see,
the sun flames. Mountains
greater than mountains.
Under a salmon sky
we open the door to the water.

TRIPTYCH

I

HEARTLAND

Crickets slowly fill the night
with slivers of the moon.
I watch a tree outside my window
draw life from our living earth.
The soil trembles and still
people keep coming: American refugees,
the hungry Irish, that long
dark line of escaped slaves.

Each carries a thimble of fire.
Each measures his world
with the feathers of a sparrow.
Midsummer. White stars cast down salt
to fill the caves of the heart.
In this season of witches
water cries out from the clear
wells at dawn.

II

THE MAP OF THE MIDWEST

When the harvest comes
friction turns
corn to lightning;

rain falls darkly
through wounded cottonwoods,
scattering branches

to the black earth.
Unfolding a map
of the Midwest

I see its net of roads,
cities I have never
visited.

I am a foreigner
yet, in an odd way,
have always lived here.

The thunder lighting up
the shattered sky
rolls a thousand miles.

III

AUTUMN RETURNS

A day drunk on yellow
tumbles from the clear sky.
Carp rise slowly
the black river
filling their mouths.

Across the floodplain
loosestrife and goldenrod
bend under a clamour
of migrating birds
their songs lost on the wind.

Bewildered Loyalists advance
beating the air with iron bells.
Generations later
their voices retain
an American flatness

cut with harsh intolerance,
with their abiding fear.
In these Midwest fields
pale bones float
brittle in the harvest cold.

IN HARVEST QUIET

Woodstock floats
on a sea of goldenrod
broken only by asters
scattered along a railway cut.

The flowers are blue shadow
like that hawk
circling the elevators,
or the blur of a passing freight.

When the harvest is finished
implements are shut away —
the scent of barn dust,
machine oil, lingers.

It is then a sharpness
drifts in on the Prairie wind
and glides like a raptor
suspended at sunset

midway between
the thin pale blue of heaven
and our darkening smoke-blue earth,
waiting to fall.

TIMESWEEP

Fingers of rain
slip in off Lake Huron
to cloak my garden,
hiding potatoes, garlic, those slim green onions
within a web of mist.
Concord grapes ripen with a slow blush.

Everywhere the mystery continues.
People die or fade to nothing,
old streets
                    change,
plywood covers rows of schoolroom windows
where once
sunlight stained an afternoon yellow.

Milkweed and thistle
spread out from along a WPA wall,
replace a knotted yew
that used to guard
the flagpole.

Already autumn patterns this Midwest town;
red leaves
spot and fall from sugar maples.
In steady rain
waves of clouds break
where rivers run.

FIRST LIGHT

Aspens appear from autumn mists
their boughs yellowing
under northern clouds.

The sound of a creek
still hidden in darkness
comes through the open window.

We lie quietly in bed
enrapt by the coolness
of early dawn.

THREE SMALL POEMS FOR AUTUMN

After twenty years
my thoughts still return home
with the autumn wind.

Valley of the Conestogo:
the river a blue scar
through cleared fields.

Under a crown of crows
the maple lights
the whole sky.

HOMAGE TO CARL SANDBURG

I AUTUMN NUMBERS

In late September
a coolness comes on the night wind
turning the first maples to gold.

. .
. .

The rushbeds stand silent
where mallards hid bright families
among curved green shadows.

. .
. .

Across this heartland of red silk corn
slow rivers draw a deeper blue
from the autumn sky.

. .
. .

Almost at midnight,
almost overhead —
the ghost-light of Andromeda
falls through two million years.

II FERNS

Ferns dance on the wind along a split-log fence.
They keep spring's slow green throughout the furnace
days of summer when flares of sunlight flick
between the boughs of sugar maples.

Even in the relentless heat the ferns are a cool
thought holding the memory of spring.
Under the shadows of spreading trees they think and
dream that dark scent of moist earth piled high
behind the turning ploughs.

III LAMENT

Under a half-moon
the city is a shifting patchwork
of quicksilver shadows
strung on a Prairie wind.

Long into the night's pale hours
the wind repeats the corn's dry song
of fields bleached
by sharp harvest skies.

The voice in the stalks
is a lament born of
that flat land beyond
the Mississippi. Like a dark river

it reaches through the night
and goes quietly leaving
a yellow silence where
darkness pools and runs.

OCTOBER SUNDAY AT THE COVE

I

Maple and oak stain the water red;
I watch their colour shift
around the still surfaces of stones
where a dry creek enters the cove.

II

All afternoon things happen around me:
small animals I can never see
root in fallen leaves; fish leap
from their dark homes below.

III

I do nothing but sit quietly
while hidden lives rise
and fall about me. The heron
has yet to follow the kingfishers south.

IV

We must meet hidden travellers
wherever we journey. The cove is dead calm.
From within God's blue silence
an osprey's piercing call.

STAGHORN

Into the chill of an October sky
this sumac casts its scarlet heart.

Iridescent leaves light cold fields
where beaten stubble mixes with pale grass.

Its limbs are a bonfire set by
the numb white fingers of an early frost.

BRANTS

On a crook
        of blue water

small black geese
    pause
in their migration

      to the Chesapeake.

They float
        where cold currents
    dive
through shadows
    of cut-bank vines.

Brants dot
        the autumn river
as it flows
  among reeds

      and
    the season's
        first frost.

THE RIVER IN EARLY OCTOBER

The river, which had been slow and shallow all summer, runs fuller now, its waters dark and fast. Bits of foam rush downstream as if the call of the autumn sea grew stronger each day. Long grasses, their stalks deep in the risen liquid, are yellow where the river cuts a wide curve through a pasture with two white mares.

For the first time in months the scent of woodsmoke drifts sharp through still air. The river has shaken the sloth of summer; a red leaf falls to the surface to be immediately swept into the swirling descent.

Everything moves lower; bullrushes, burdened with the season, bend toward their roots; the sap retreats in trees that overhang the bank. In its own way the yellow birch welcomes this changed mood, relinquishing thousands of leaves to the same downward motion, urgently and without regret. And the cherries have long abandoned most of their leaves; they flee like adolescents eager to leave home for the city.

When evening comes, moisture rises from the surface. These vapours, white in white moonlight, ignore the movements of the river despite being almost within its wet embrace. By midnight only two things remain: the mist, still lingering among sedges, and the sound of darkness descending into this world of matter and loss.